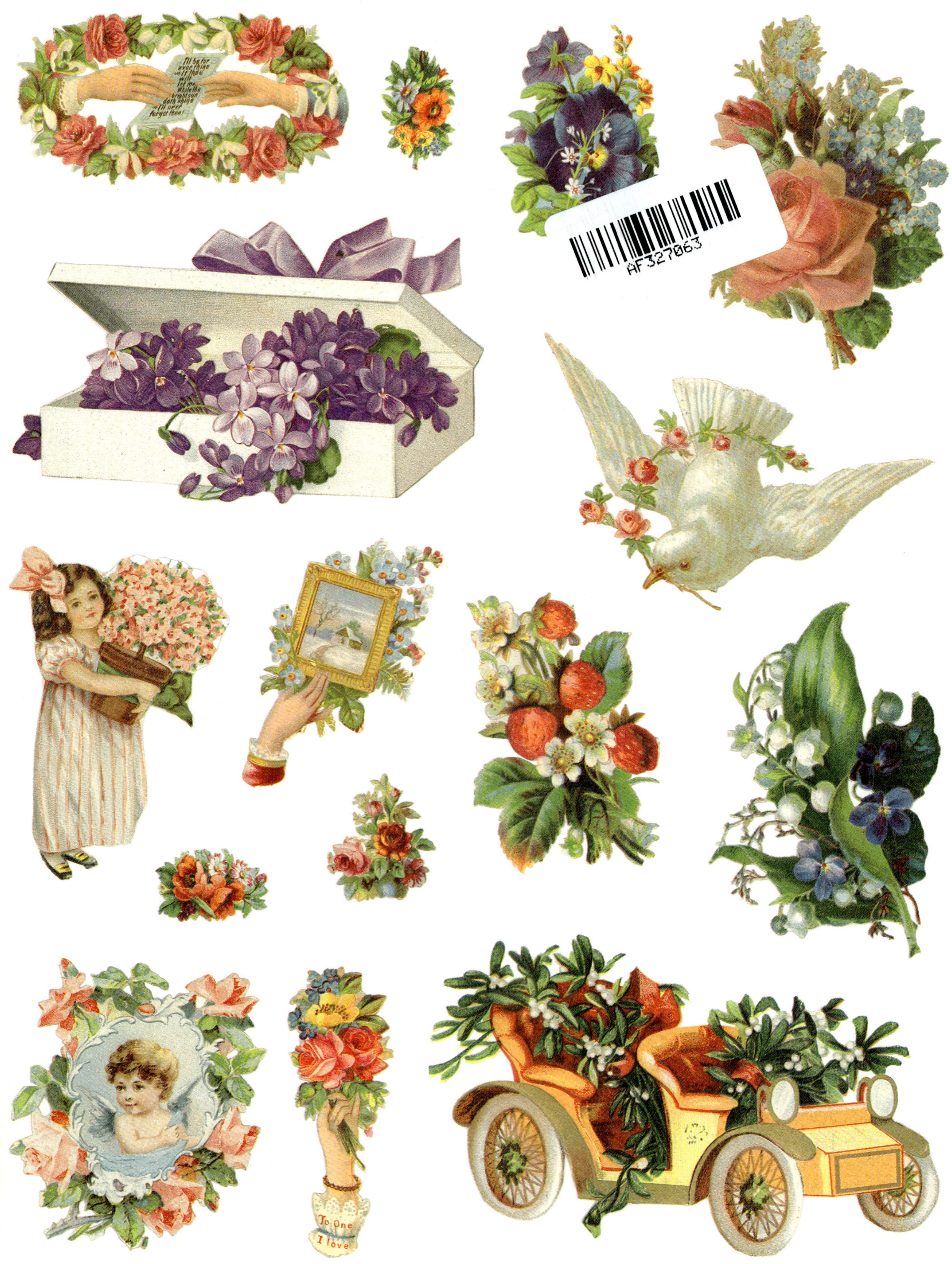

Plate 1

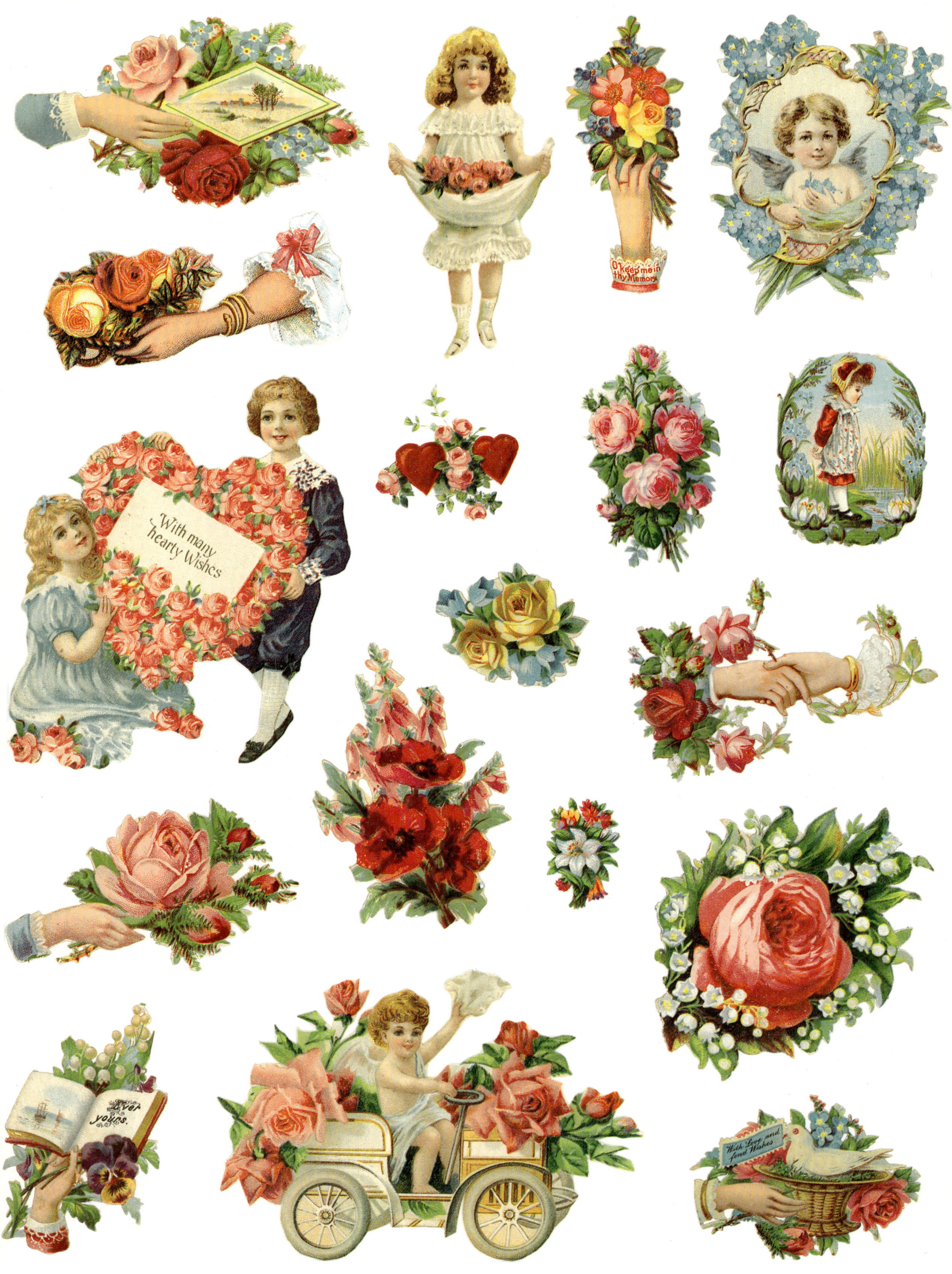

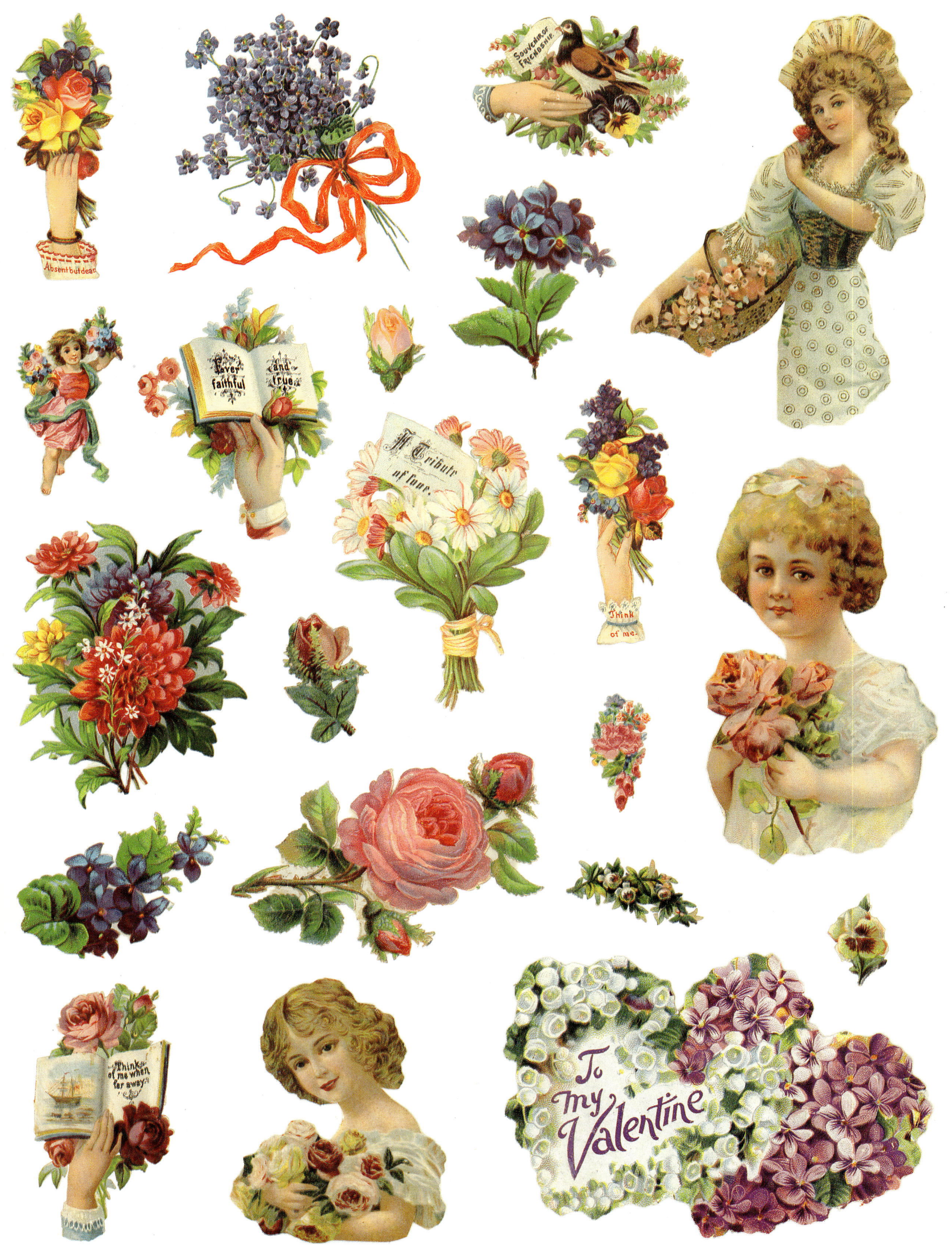
Absent but dear
Souvenir of Friendship
Ever faithful and true
A Tribute of love.
Think of me.
Think of me when far away
To my Valentine

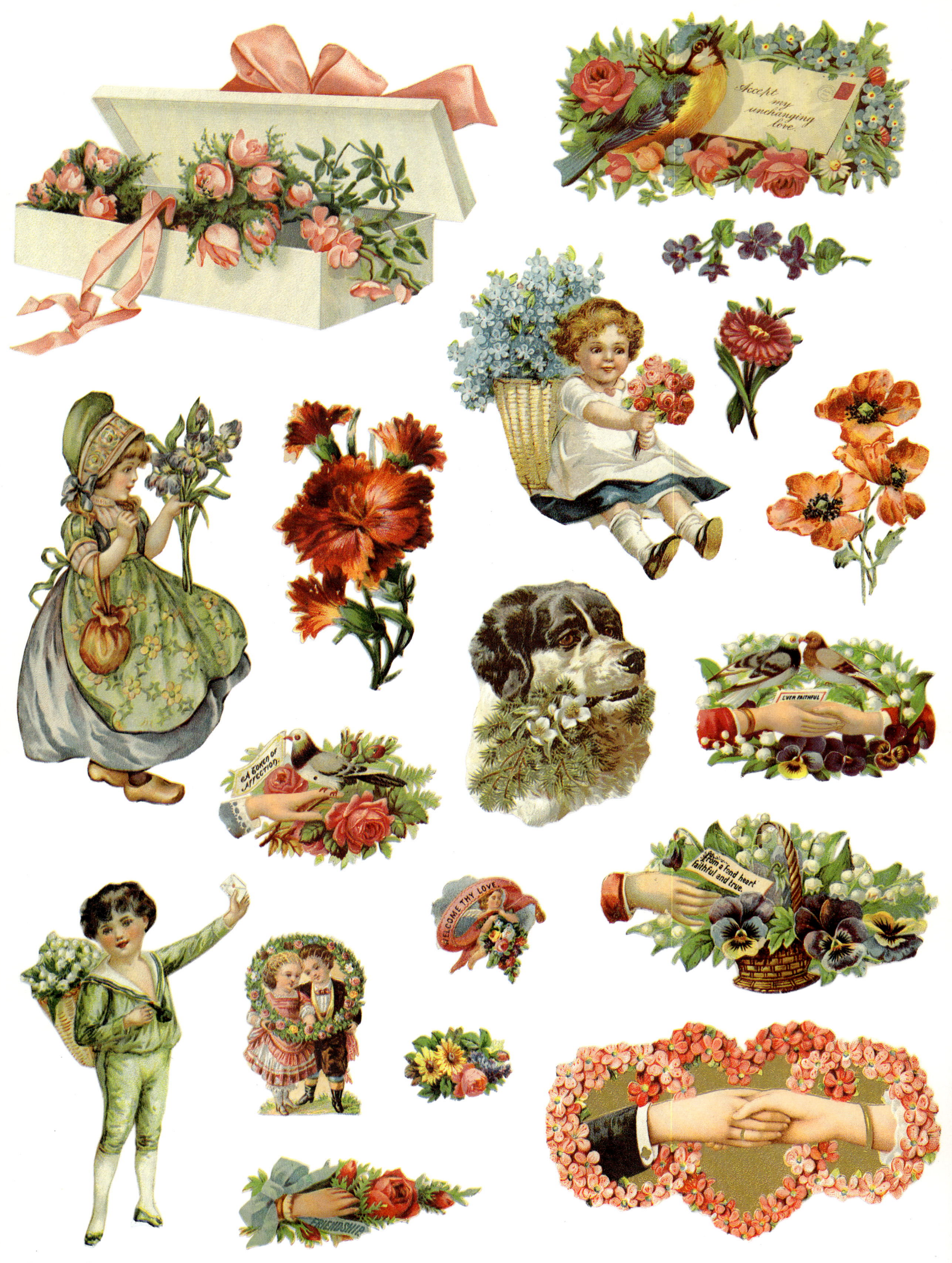
Accept my unchanging love.
A TOKEN OF AFFECTION.
EVER FAITHFUL
WELCOME THY LOVE.
From a fond heart faithful and true.
FRIENDSHIP

PLATE 4

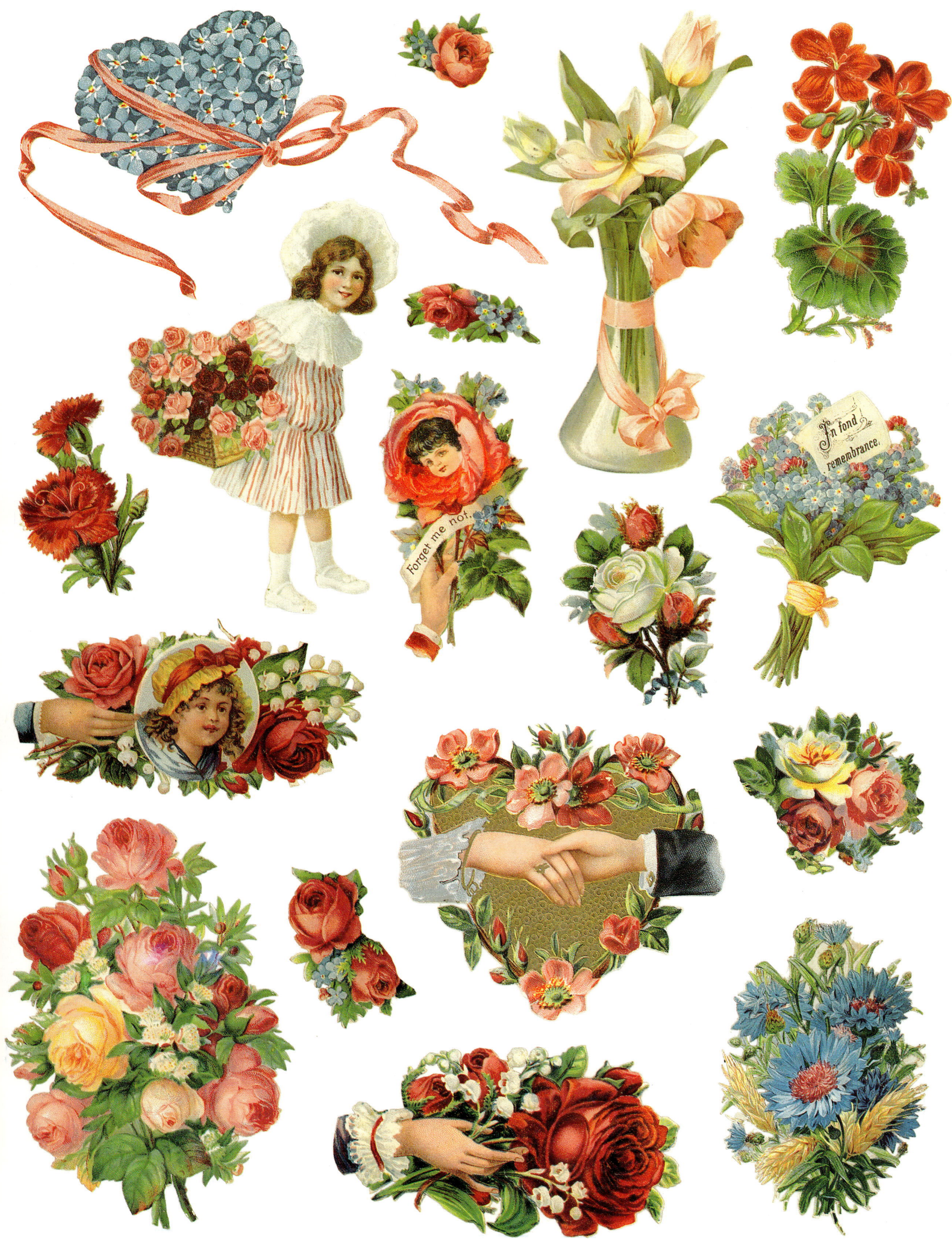
In fond
remembrance.
Forget me not.

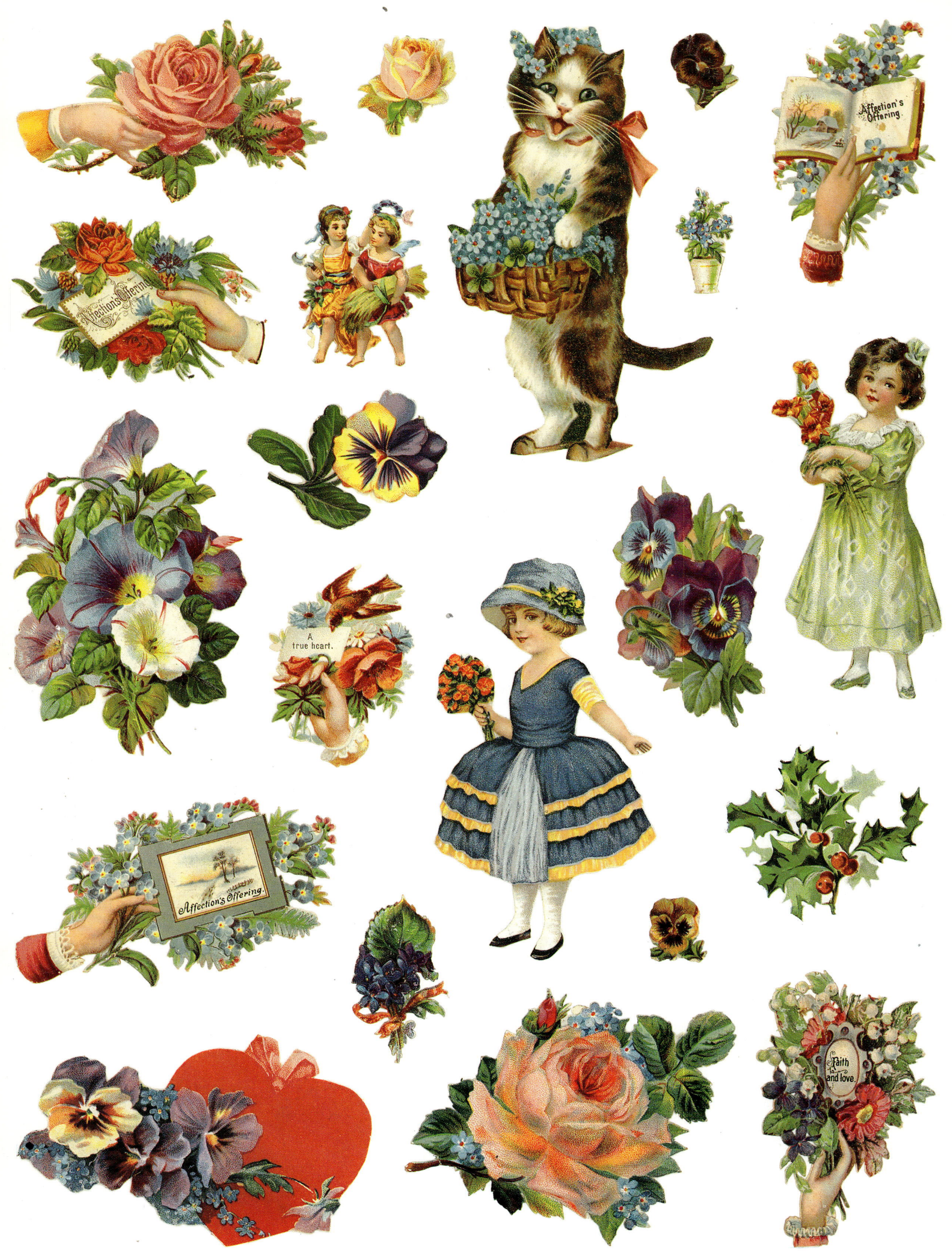

Affection's Offering.
Affection's Offering
A true heart.
Affection's Offering.
Faith and love.

PLATE 6

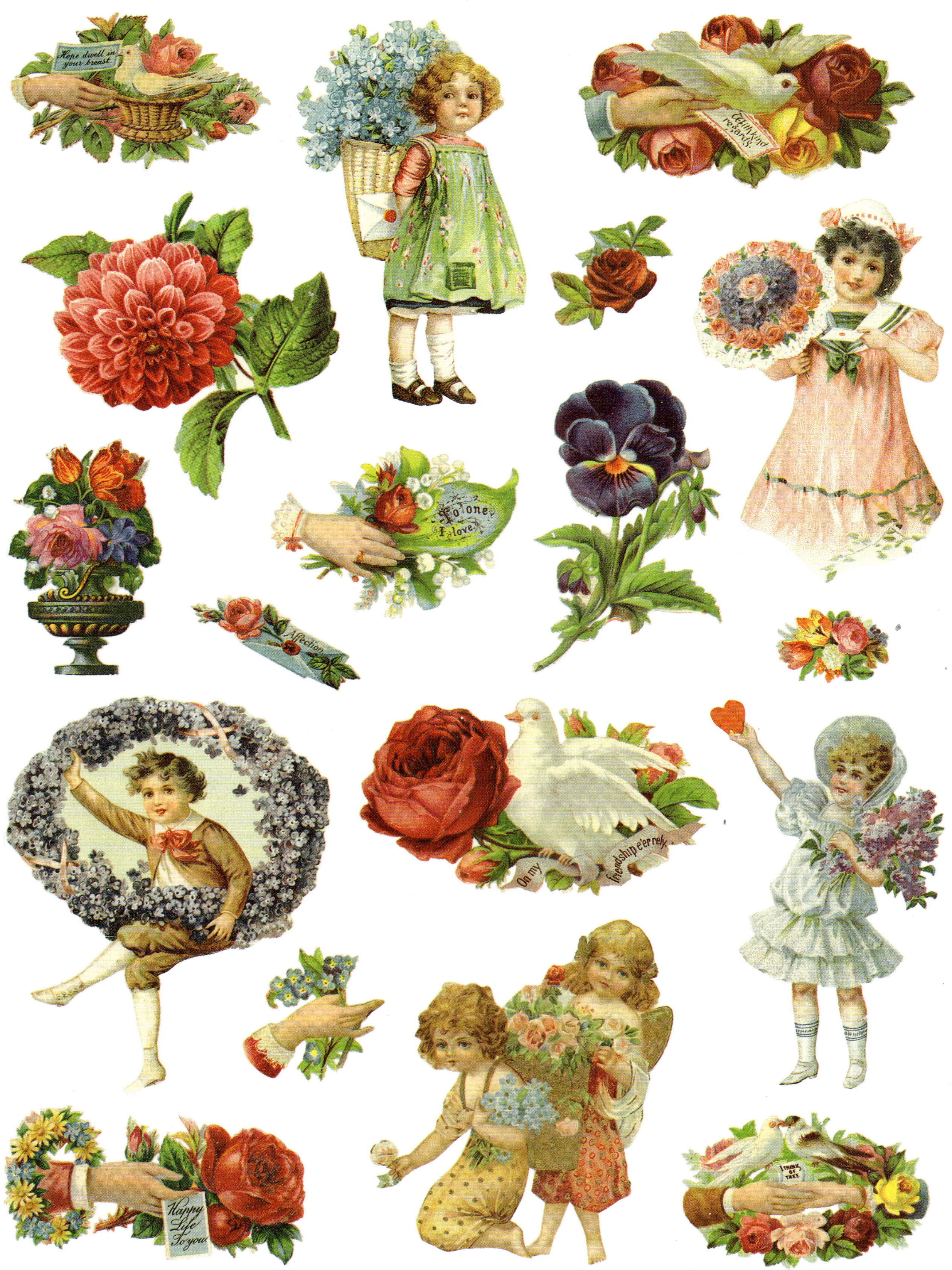
Hope dwell in your breast.
With Kind regards.
To one I love
Affection
On my
friendship e'er reign.
Happy Life to you.
Think of thee.

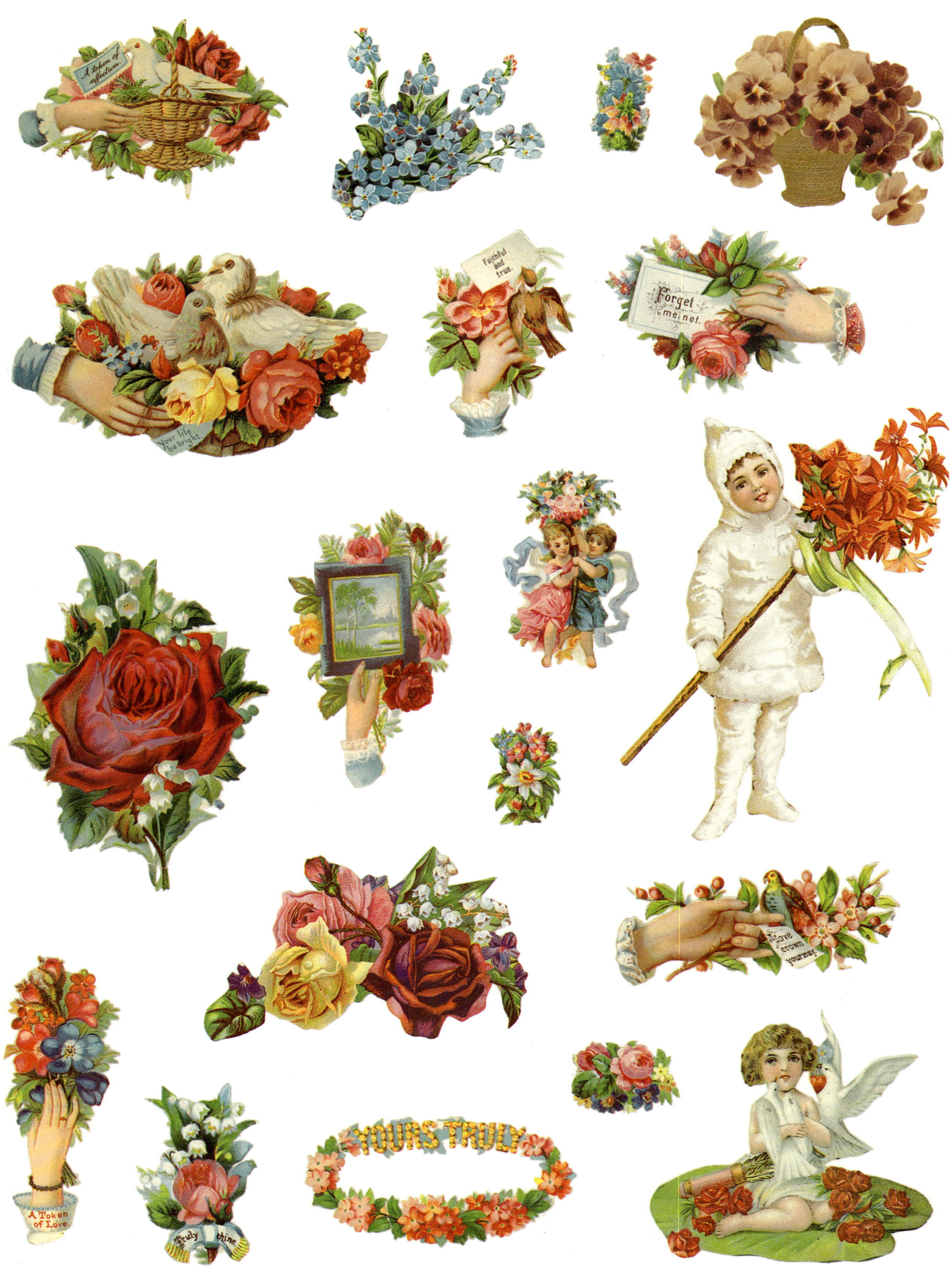

A Token of affection.
Faithful and true.
Forget me not.
Your life be bright!
Love crown your may!
A Token of Love.
Truly thine
YOURS TRULY

PLATE 8

think of thee
To
My Sweetheart
From
Postage
Two Kisses
FRIENDSHIP
SWEET REMEMBRANCE
Constancy
A true heart.

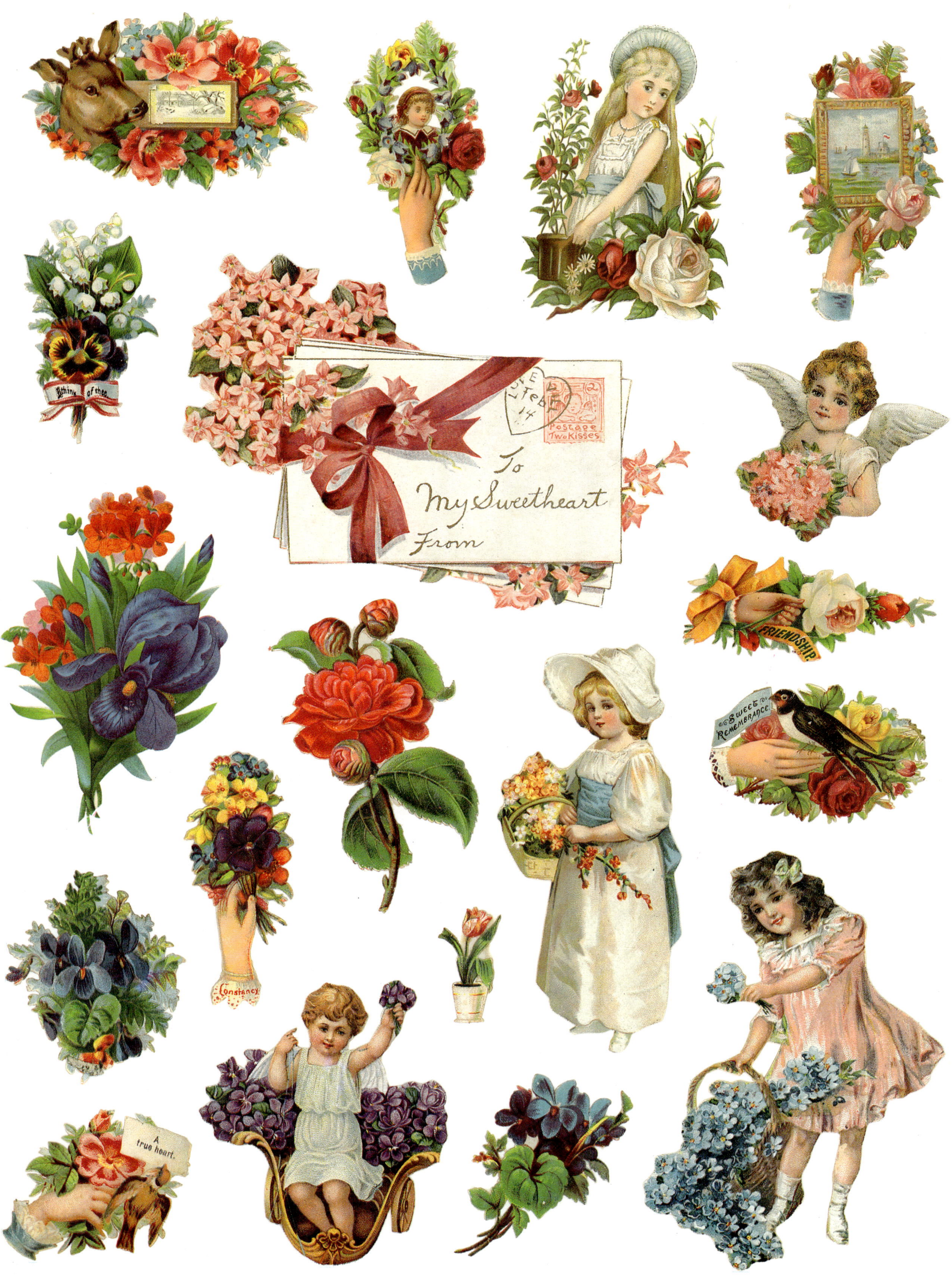

PLATE 9

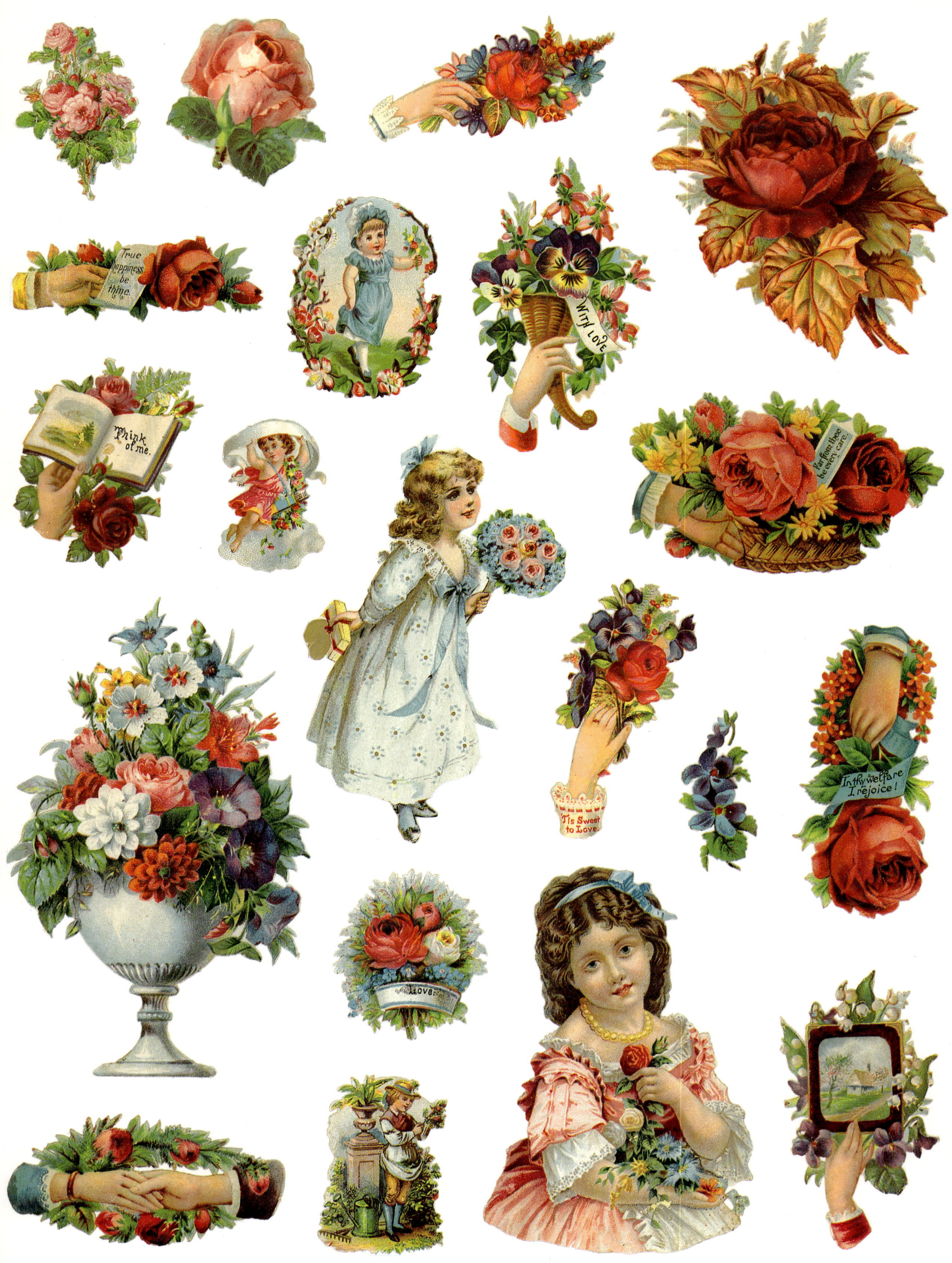

True Happiness be thine.
With Love
Think of me.
Tis Sweet to Love.
In thy welfare I rejoice!

PLATE 10

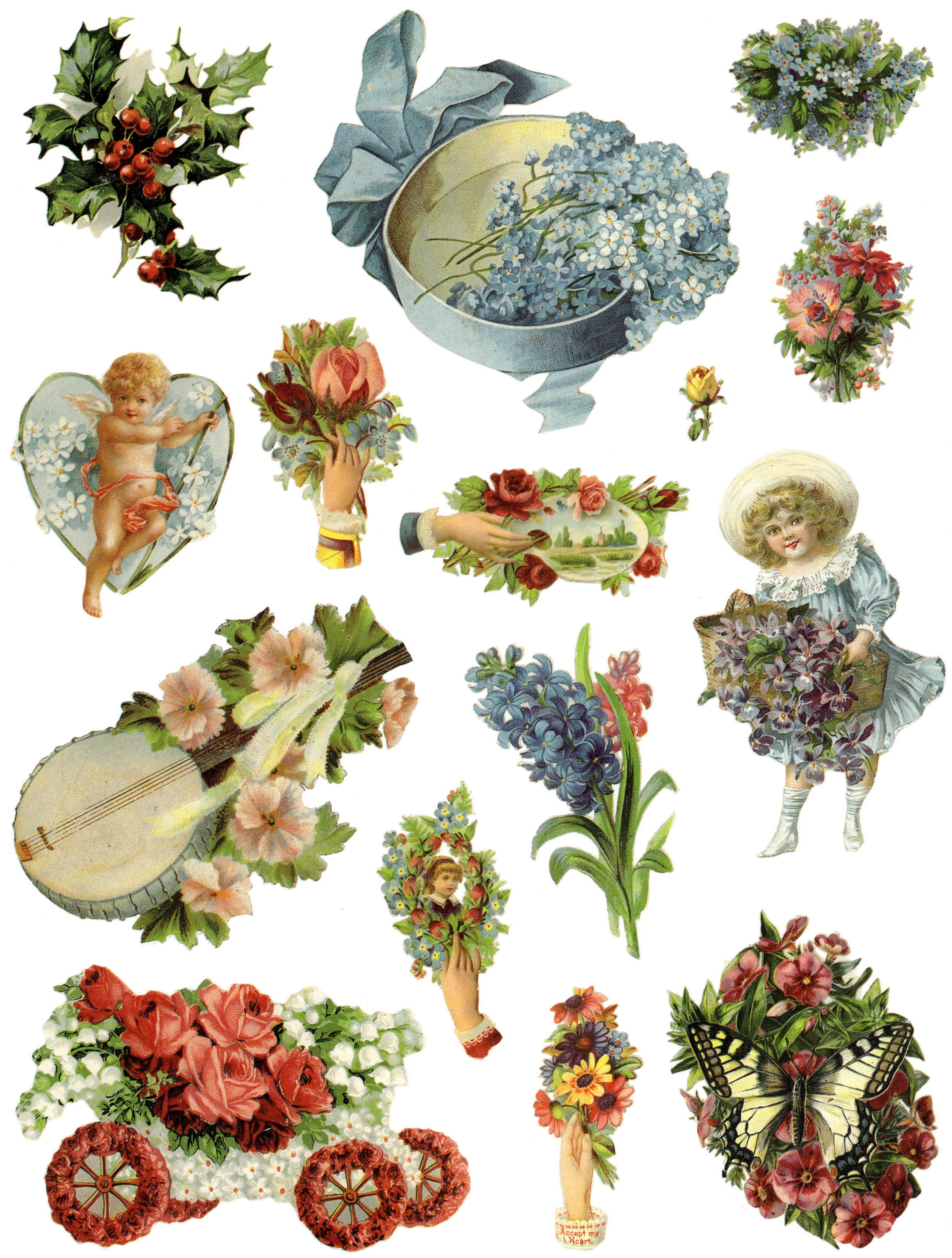

PLATE 11

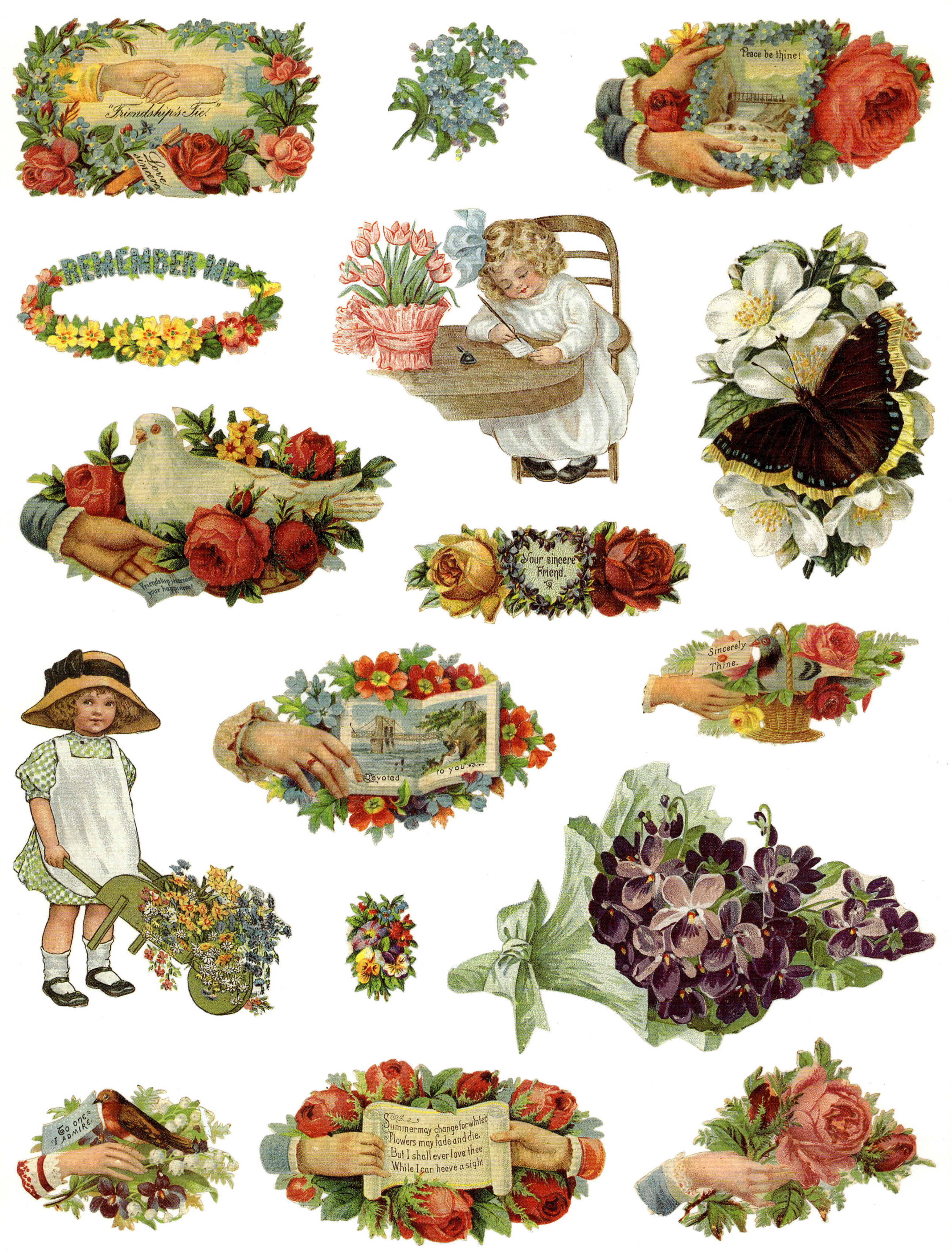

"Friendship's Tie."
Love sincere
Peace be thine!
REMEMBER ME
Friendship increase your happiness!
Your sincere Friend.
Sincerely Thine.
Devoted to you.
To one I Admire.
Summer may change for winter,
Flowers may fade and die,
But I shall ever love thee
While I can heave a sigh.

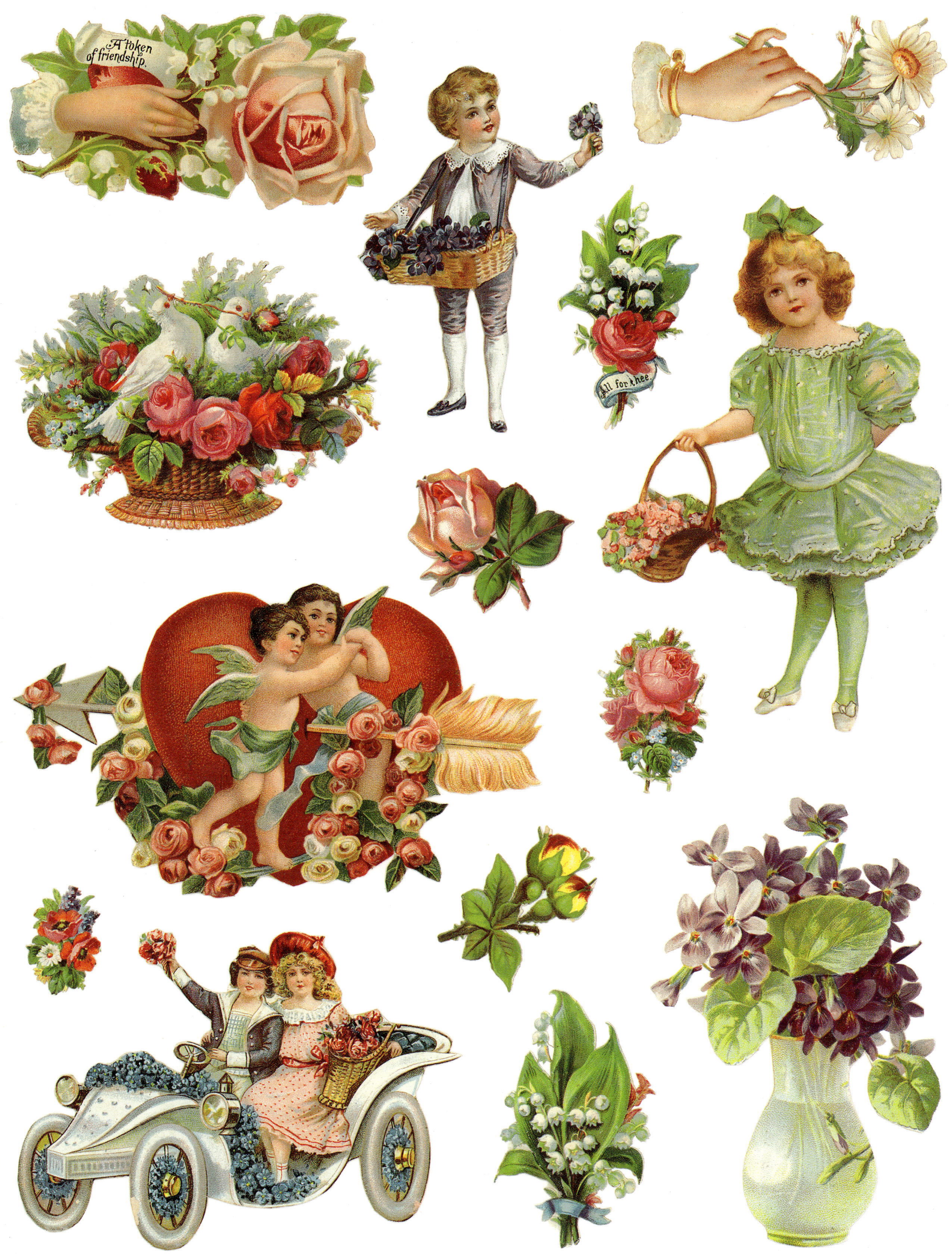

PLATE 13

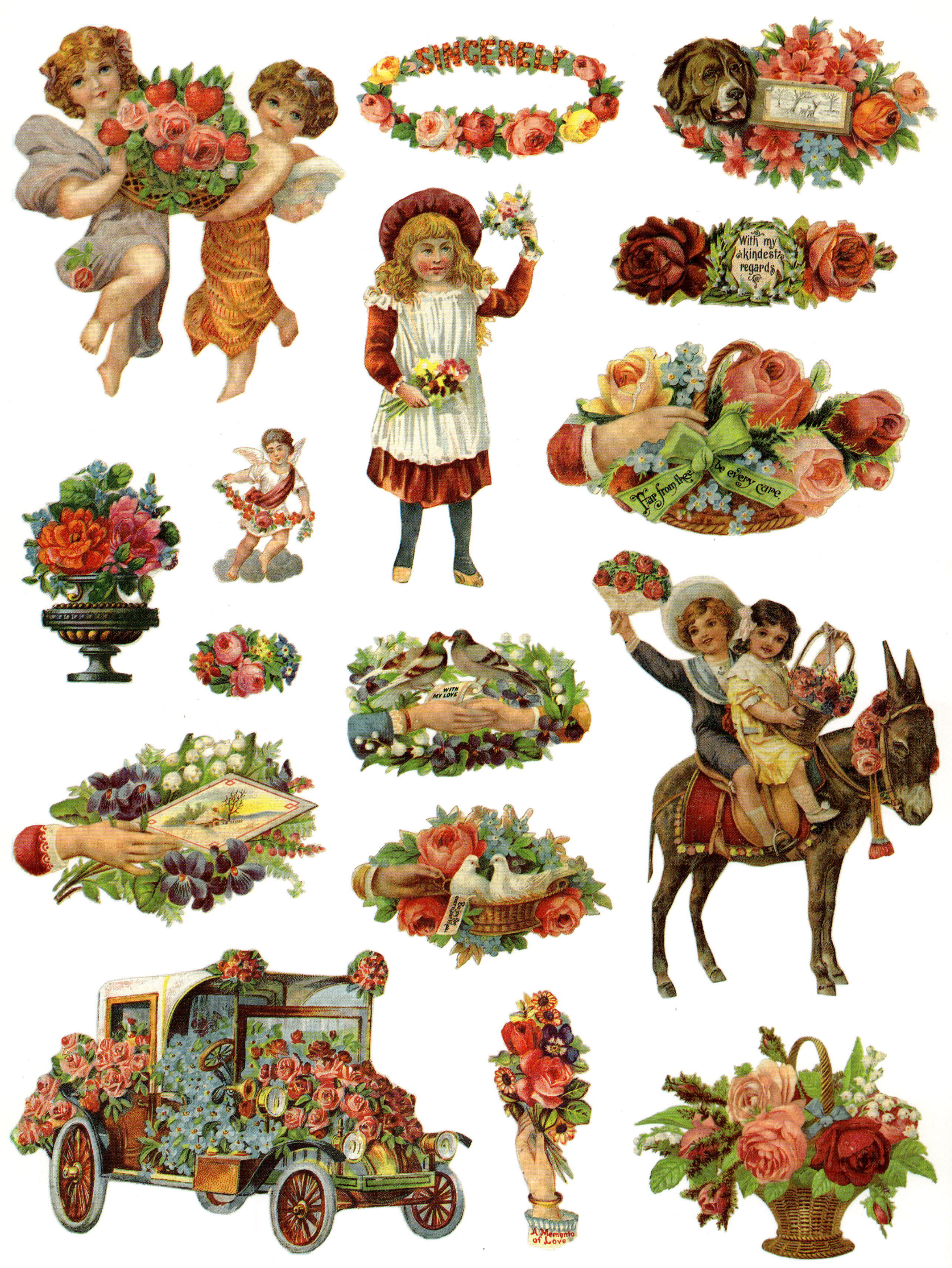

SINCERELY
With my kindest regards
WITH MY LOVE
A Memento of Love

Plate 14

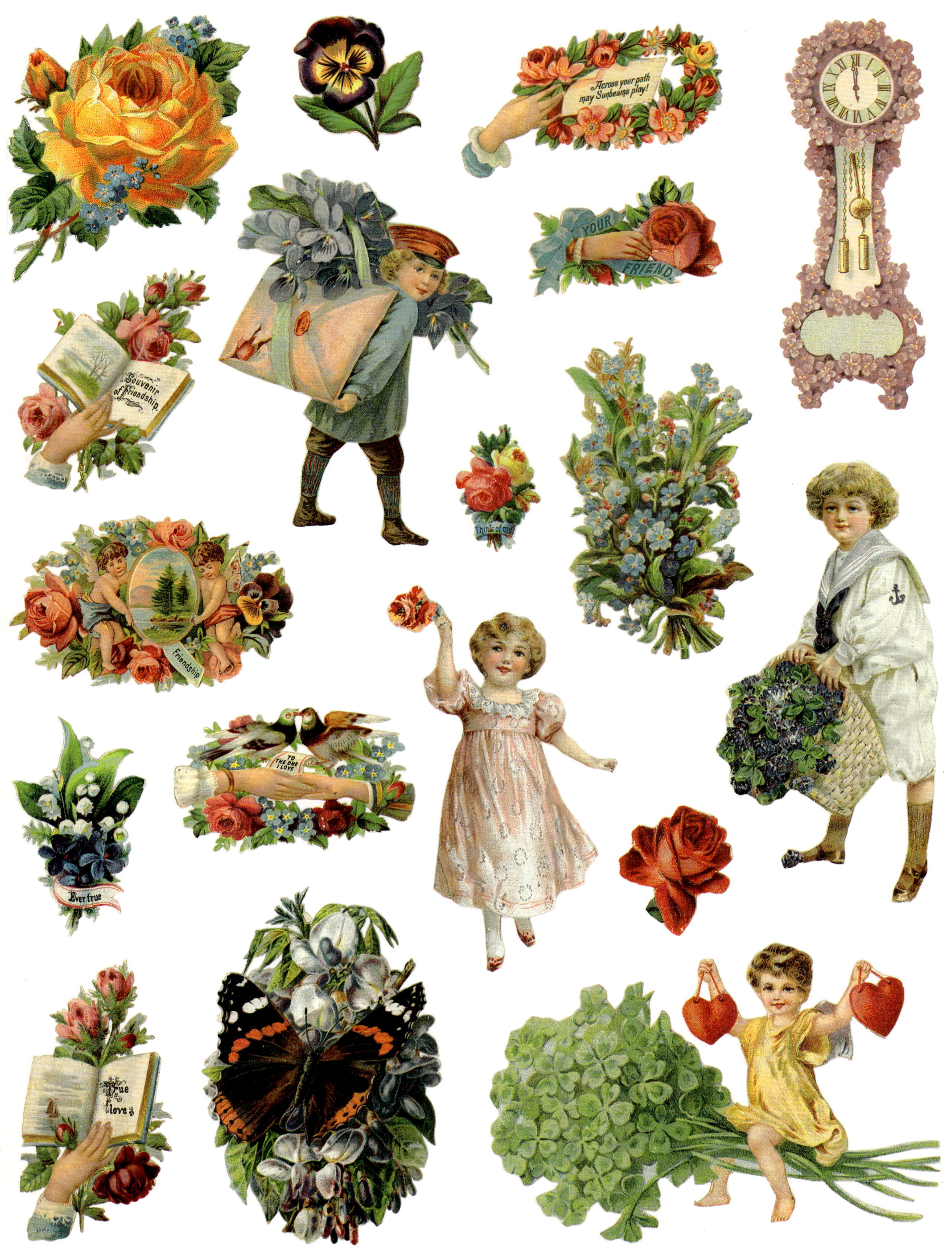

Across your path
may Sunbeams play!
YOUR FRIEND.
Souvenir of Friendship.
Think of me!
Friendship
TO THE ONE I LOVE
Ever true
True love

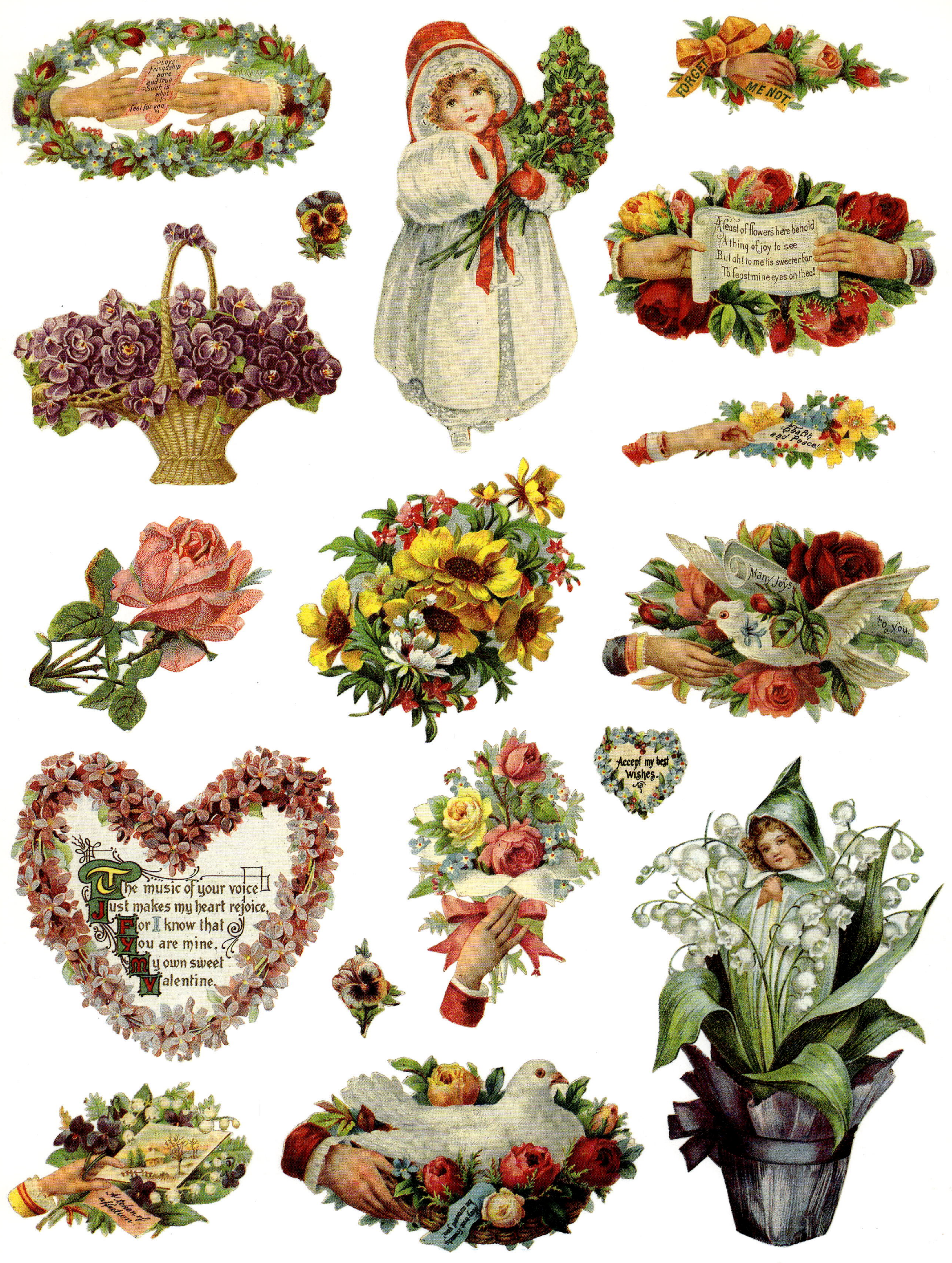

Loya Friendship pure and true Such is what I feel for you.

FORGET ME NOT.

A feast of flowers here behold
A thing of joy to see
But ah! to me 'tis sweeter far
To feast mine eyes on thee!

Health and Peace!

Many Joys to You.

Accept my best wishes.

The music of your voice
Just makes my heart rejoice,
For I know that you are mine,
My own sweet Valentine.

PLATE 16

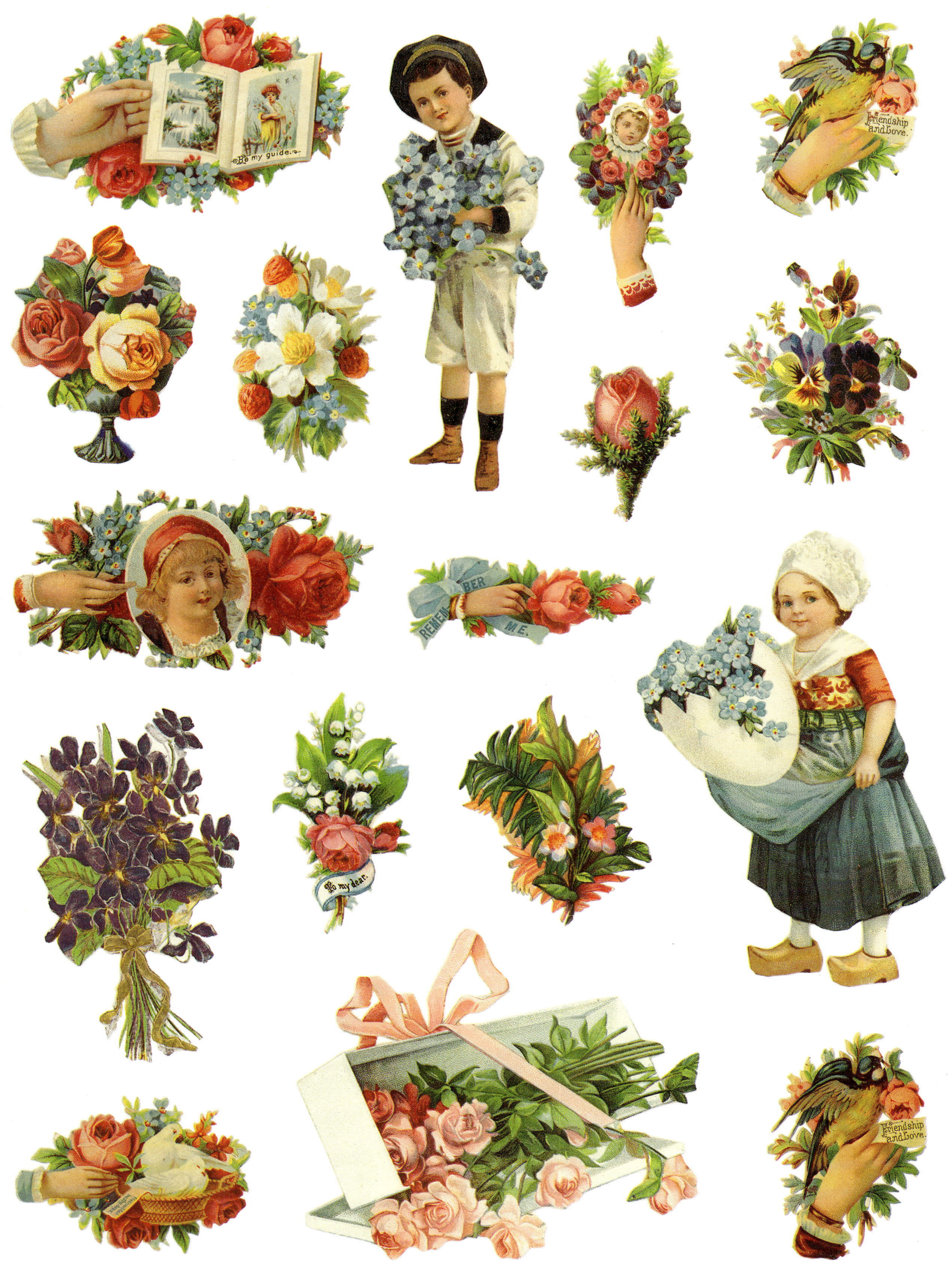

Be my guide.
Friendship and Love.
REMEMBER ME.
To my dear.
Friendship and Love.

PLATE 17

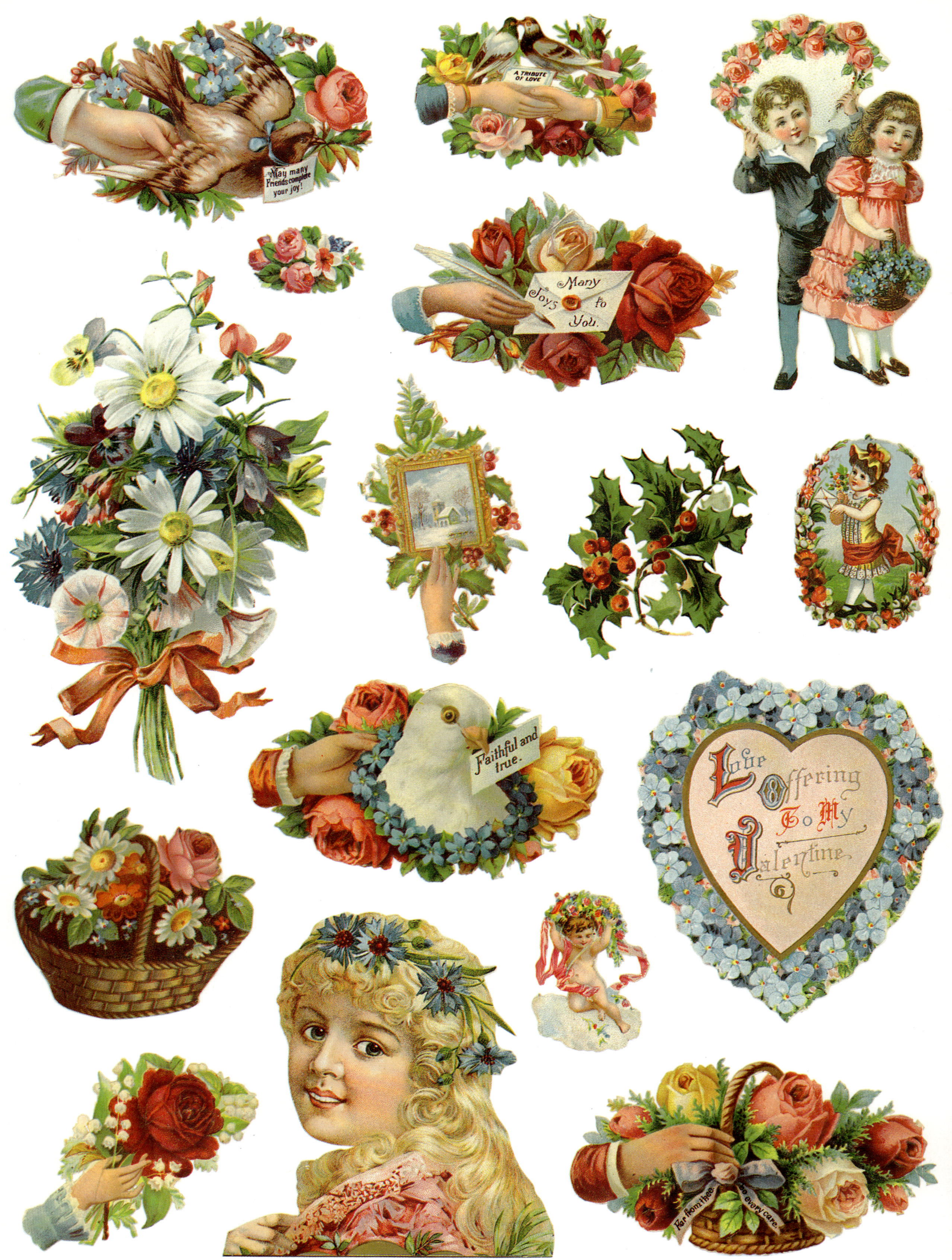
May many Friends complete your joy!
A TRIBUTE OF LOVE
Many Joys to You.
Faithful and true.
Love Offering To My Valentine

Plate 18

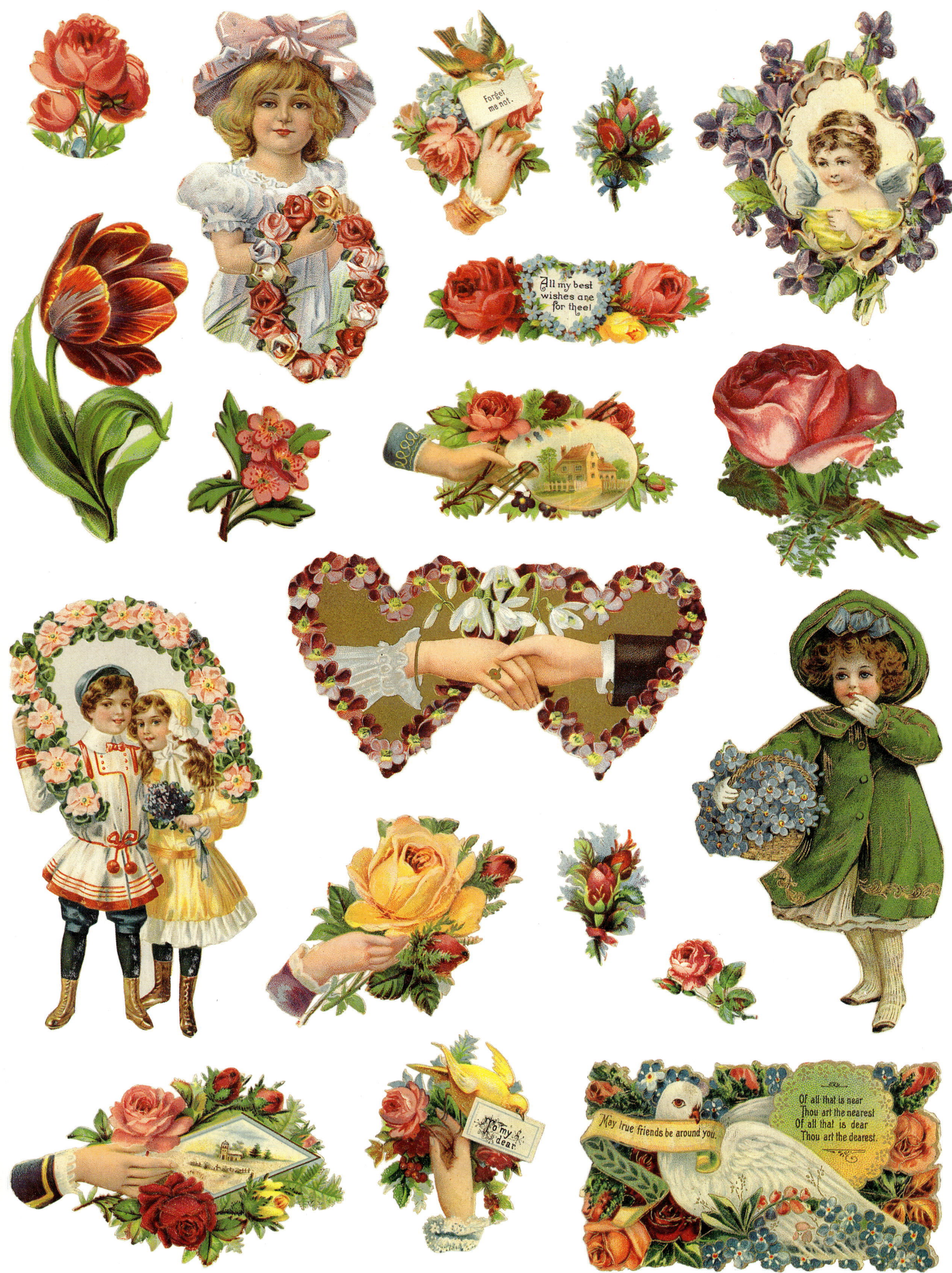

Forget me not.
All my best wishes are for thee!
To my dear
May true friends be around you.
Of all that is near Thou art the nearest Of all that is dear Thou art the dearest.

PLATE 19

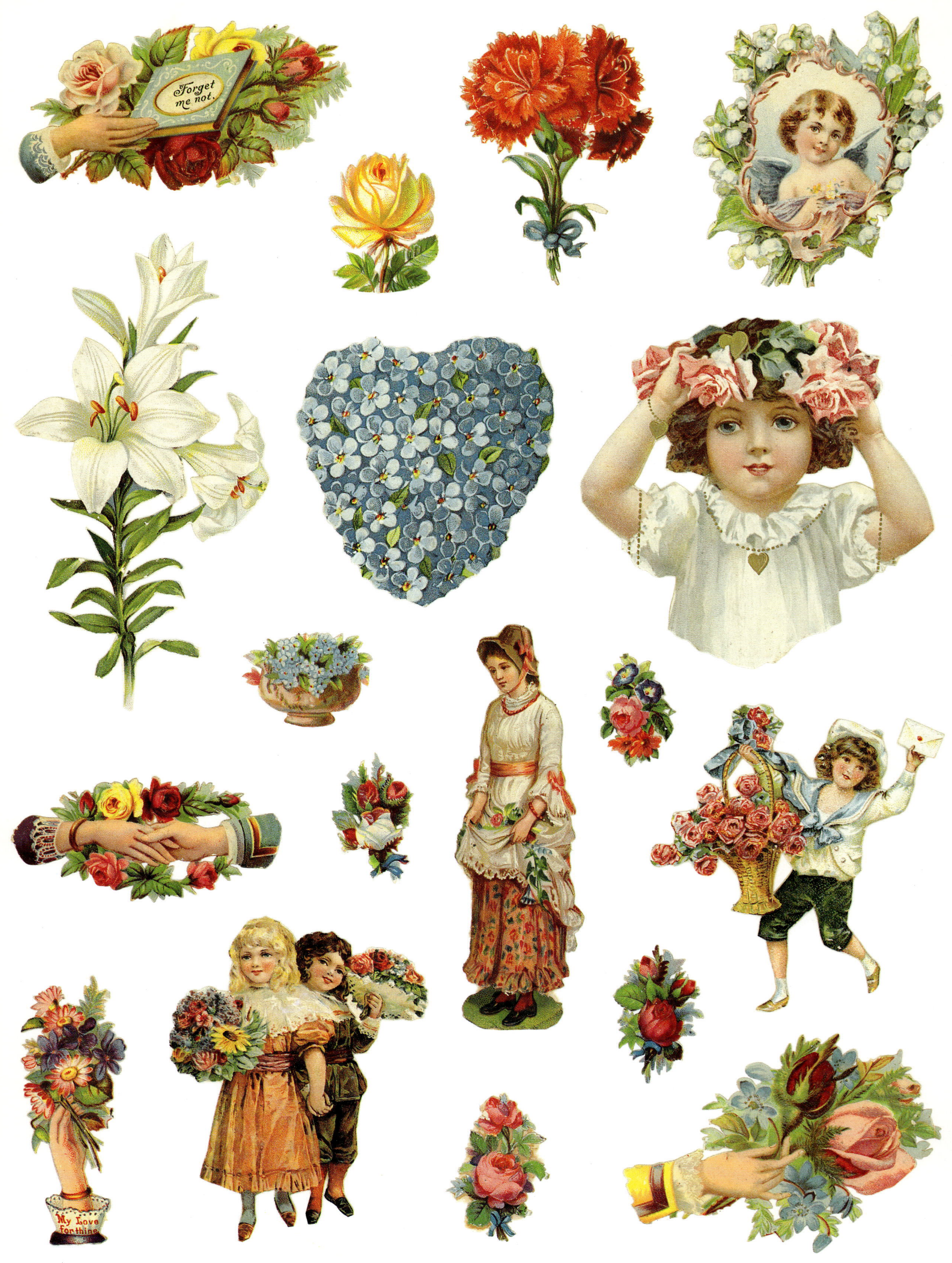

PLATE 20

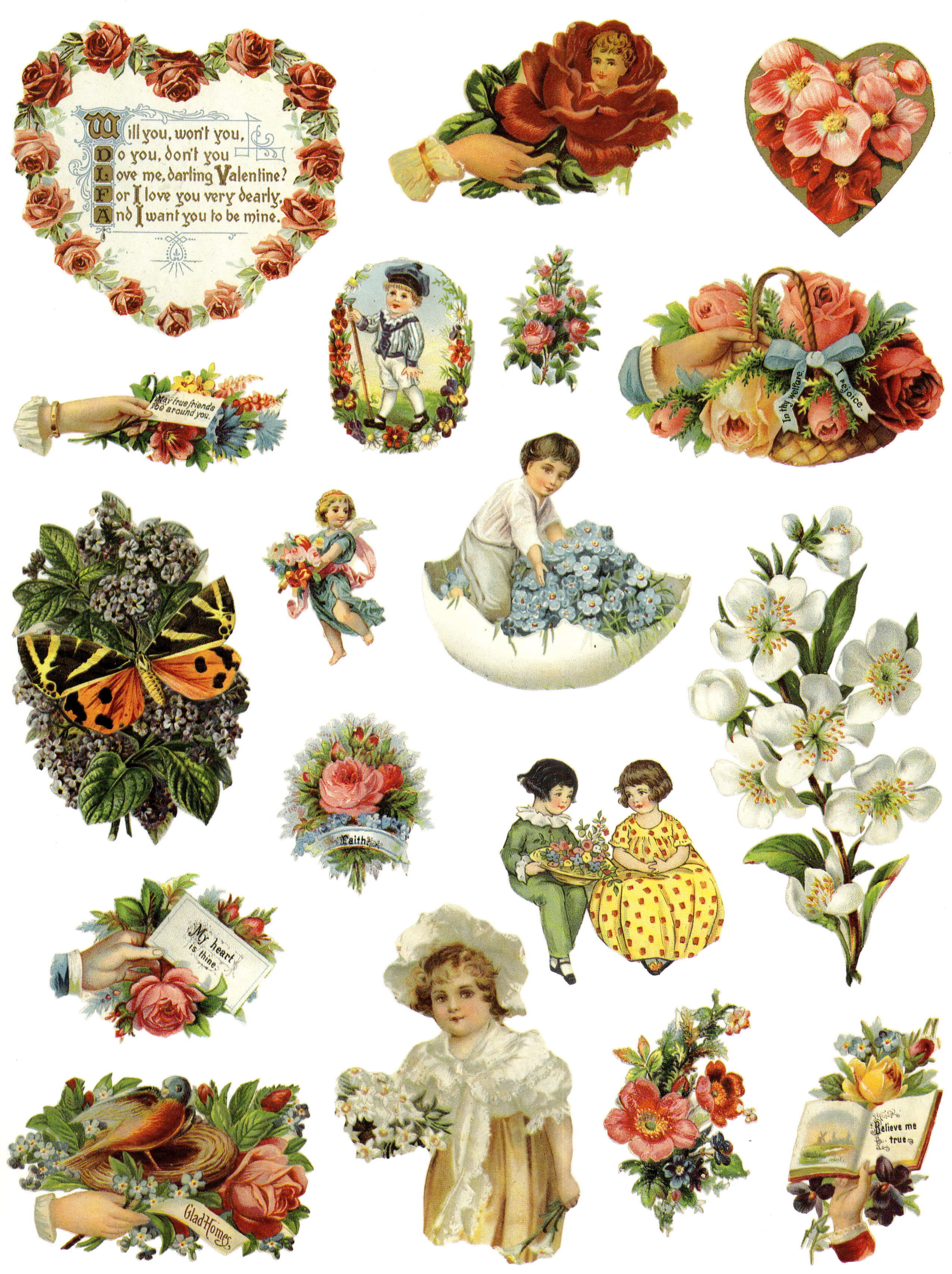

Will you, won't you, Do you, don't you love me, darling Valentine? For I love you very dearly, And I want you to be mine.
May true friends be around you.
In thy welfare I rejoice.
Faith
My heart is thine.
Glad Homes.
Believe me true

PLATE 21

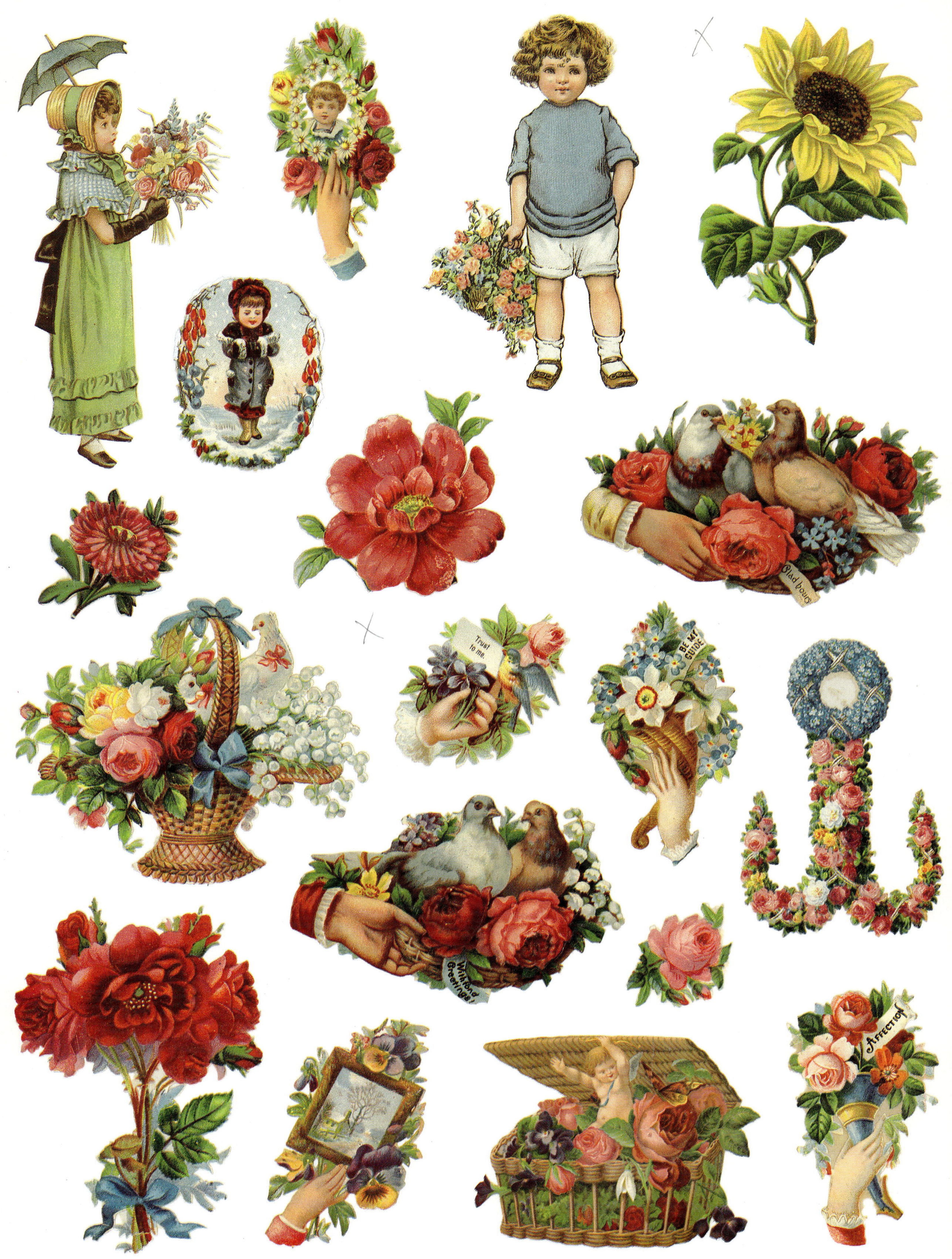

PLATE 22

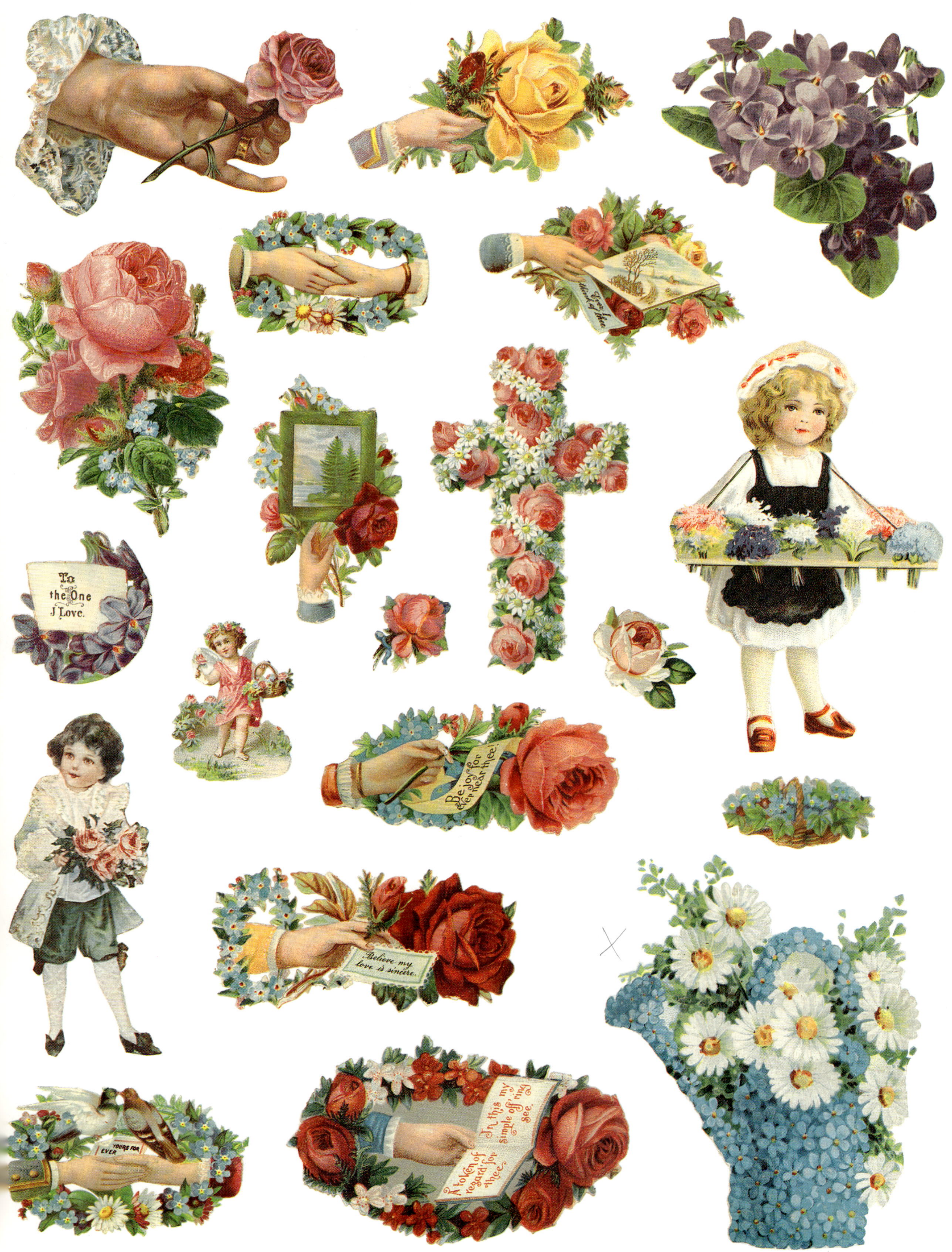
To the One I Love.
Be joy forever near thee
Believe my love is sincere.
YOURS FOR EVER
In this my simple offering see
A token of regard for thee

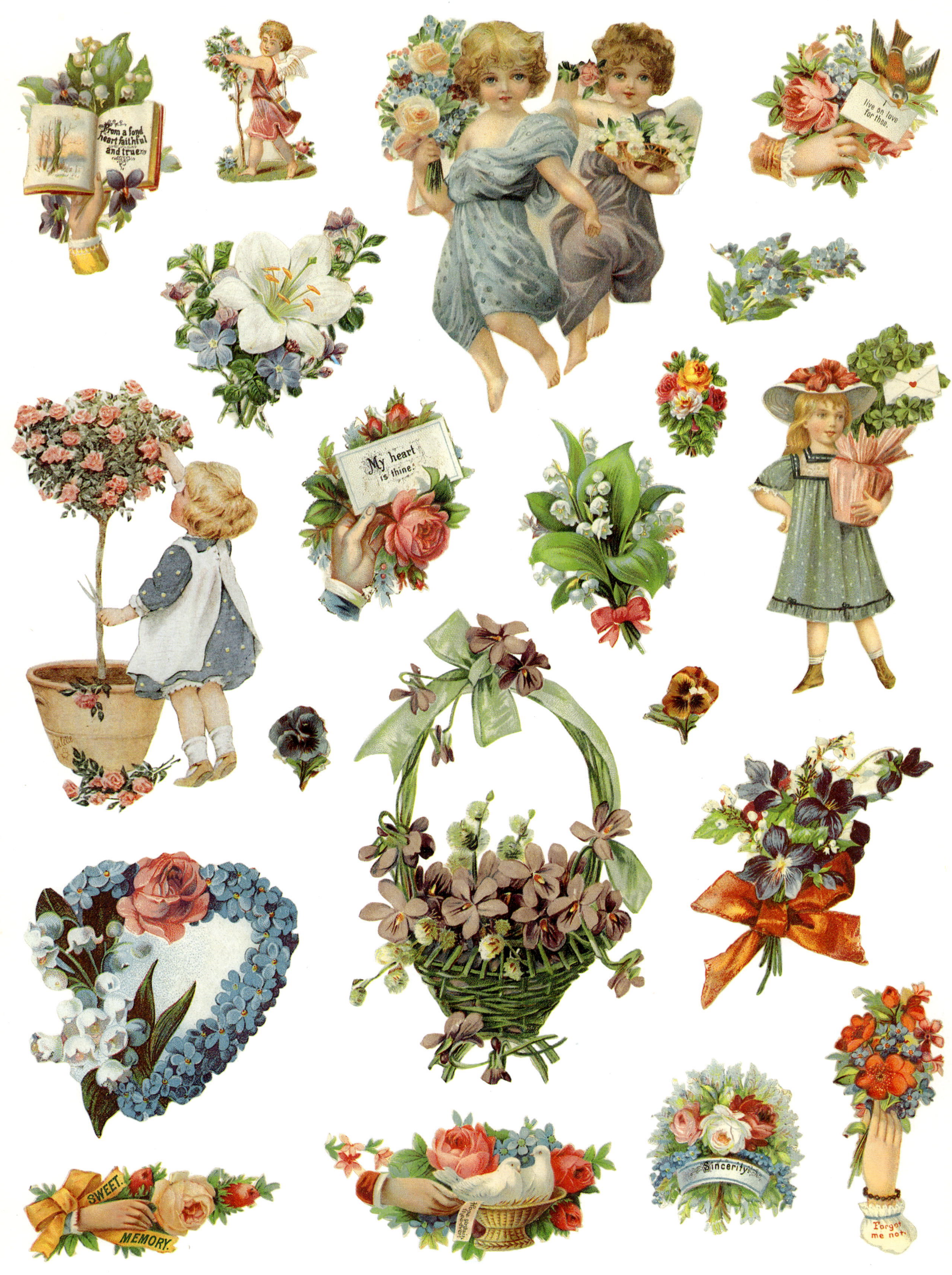
From a fond heart faithful and true
I live on love for thee.
My heart is thine.
SWEET.
MEMORY.
Sincerity
Forget me not.

PLATE 24